CW00553509

Southborough and High Brooms
in old picture postcards

by A.M. Macfarlane

European Library ZALTBOMMEL/THE NETHERLANDS

GB ISBN 90 288 6445 8

© 1997 European Library – Zaltbommel/The Netherlands

Introduction

Southborough stands on the northern edge of the High Weald Area of Outstanding Natural Beauty, along and astride the main road between Tonbridge and Tunbridge Wells. Writing in 1885 about the town as a potential health resort, a local resident physician, Dr. E. Paget Thurstan, remarked on the advantages of its position above the River Medway and he enthused about the Common and the quality of the air and water, including the chalybeate spring at Stemps Farm.

From Norman times, Southborough was simply the southern borough or tithing of Tonbridge, lying within the Lowy or domain of Tonbridge Castle. Much of the area south of the Medway at Tonbridge formed part of a great hunting chase, South Frith, and the earliest occupied hamlets locally would have been established just outside the boundary fence of that Royal preserve.

From the middle of the 16th century, the forests began to be cleared to provide fuel for iron-ore smelting, and the clearings began to be used for agriculture, which provided most of the work available until the mid-19th century. During the 18th century, however, many people in Southborough benefitted greatly by housing and catering for the many visitors to the emerging spa town of Tunbridge Wells, before that place was able to provide such accommodation itself. Also, from about 1850, the town achieved some fame as a centre for cricket ball making and a surprising number of men worked to meet the demand. Right up to the last decade of the 19th century, the town was still in the civil parish of Tonbridge. Then, under the Local Government Act of 1894, an Urban District Council was constituted. This arrangement lasted until 1 April 1974, when the town was absorbed into the Borough of Tunbridge Wells, but it retained a Town Council and the then Chairman of the Urban District Council became the first Town Mayor.

Described in Victorian times as a 'growing' town, Southborough has actually grown in a patchy way. Apart from individual farms and houses dotted around, development up to the middle of the 19th century tended to be on and around the Common. It was not until after 1860 that much expansion took place in the southern part of the town and when in the 1880s what became known as 'New Town' spread west of London Road, there was still a buffer zone of fields between the two halves of the town, each area being served by its own shops, inns and churches.

The hamlet of High Brooms originally consisted of the cottages occupied by the employees of various brick-making firms, especially the renowned High Brooms Brick and Tile Company (1885-1968), and the Tunbridge Wells Gas Company. For some years, Tunbridge Wells and Southborough disputed financial responsibility for it, but it was part of the parish of St. Peter, Southborough, until its own fine church was built in 1902, and the curve of the railway line to the east clearly draws High Brooms into the embrace of Southborough.

Since the end of the Second World War, the break-up of two extensive estates made land available for much building; on the old Broomhill Estate, large numbers of council houses were put up, whilst on the Great Bounds Estate another quantity of larger houses was built for sale.

From having been largely self-sufficient in shops and facilities until the 1960s, Southborough now looks increasingly outwards to large shopping centres and to larger communities for employment, so that it is becoming more of a dormitory town, with its people commuting further afield for jobs. However, despite these distractions, Southborough retains much of the general atmosphere of a village, where people know each other, and there continues to be a spirit of togetherness.

This spirit is fostered by the Southborough Society, which records the history and activities of the community and keeps a watchful eye on any development and its effect on the quality of life in the town.

As for the material from which this book has been compiled, Southborough has been well-served by national publishers of postcards, such as F. Frith, L. Levy, Salmon, Photochrom and Valentine. However, it has also been very lucky in having several productive local publishers: Fielder & Jarrett published over 220 numbered cards and at least 25 unnumbered ones (for private customers) in the first two decades of this century; Alec Brook of Edward Street produced at least 150 postcards in the 1920s and 1930s. E.A. Sweetman published over 75 numbered cards before and after the Second World War, and H.H. Camburn, Arthur Dee and James Richards issued several more each.

The layout of this book takes the form of a strolling tour from south to north, with several diversions to outlying areas, ending at Mabledon, overlooking the Medway Valley.

Illustrations: are from the postcard collection of the author, except Nos. 74 and 75, of which copies have been kindly provided by Mr. Fred Scales, of Southborough.

1   Until the early 1960s, the first building in Southborough seen by any traveller from Tunbridge Wells would have been the little cottage on the left of this picture, which stands on the corner of Powder Mill Lane, where it joins London Road. It was the lodge of Southfield Park, an imposing mansion which ended its days as a private school but was pulled down in the 1930s. Its grounds became the playing fields of The Skinners School, Tunbridge Wells. The house visible on the right collapsed in a gale in early January 1925, possibly because the foundations had been weakened when a cellar was dug out some time after the house was built. Powder Mill Lane here forms the town boundary with Tunbridge Wells and runs away north-eastwards, eventually to form the rough boundary between Southborough and High Brooms.

Powder Mill Lane, High Brooms.   196.

2   Frederick Mules & Co., bakers, stood on the corner of Speldhurst Road and London Road from before 1880, the first in an almost continuous line of shops and traders along the western side of London Road until almost at The Weavers. Curiously, apart from two inns, there were very few shops on the eastern side of the road here. Paine, Smith, bakers, took over the business in 1929-30 and at one time had no less than three shops in Southborough. The ornamental brick wall was removed in the 1950s, to open up a car-park, and with it disappeared the first letter-box set up in the town, just visible at the right-hand end of the wall.

3   The almshouses at Gallards Close, London Road, were built in 1912 under the bequest of C.J. Gallard, a local builder, at a cost not to exceed £5,000. The three blocks of flats, totalling twenty, were intended to house eight single men, eight single women and, in the smaller central block, four married couples. The weekly rents payable in 1912 are reported as being 15/- (75p) for a married couple and 10/- (50p) for a single person. Except that the driveway seen in the picture no longer exists, they still look now much as they did when built, thanks to the care of the trustees. Actually, the scheme was originally intended to be larger but, owing to a depressed market, Mr. Gallard's estate did not realise as much as had been expected. The northern end of the plot was therefore sold off to Lloyds Bank Ltd., who built a new branch on it, and the money thus raised enabled the almshouses to be completed.

The Gallard Almshouses, Southborough.

4   On the extreme left of this picture can be seen part of the Flying Dutchman Inn, named after the winner of The Derby and St. Leger in 1849. The greengrocer next door, William Waters, was taking full advantage of the fact that he, like all the traders along London Road, owned the forecourt outside his shop. Just before the outbreak of the Second World War, the Flying Dutchman expanded to take over the greengrocer's shop, which then moved around the next corner along, into Western Road. Albert Maynard's outfitter's shop is now occupied by R.N. Carr Ltd. and further along London Road, just to the left of the horse and cart, a large projecting sign proclaims a Temperance Hotel and Restaurant.

London Road, Southborough.

33.

5   A plot of land on London Road was bought in 1866 for £175 and a house called Merton Villa was built on it. Later a single-storey addition was made to the front and, in 1871, it opened as a Temperance Hotel. In 1883, the ladies of Southborough raised money to fit it out as a good coffee tavern and library, with accommodation for the manager. In 1917, part of the dining-room was leased to the Westminster Bank Ltd. until 1942. By 1927, the coffee tavern had become a stationer's shop, which later became The Wattle Library. From 1942, The Wattle Library shared the building with the Southborough Library, but the latter moved into its present, award-winning, building in Yew Tree Road in April 1962 and its place was taken by the Public Health Department of Southborough UDC. In 1974, Southborough Stationers took over the whole premises but closed in 1995. The shop re-opened in February 1997 as a specialist sub-aqua store.

The Temperance Hotel, Southborough.

6 The Royal Victoria Hall, which was built to commemorate the Diamond Jubilee of Queen Victoria, opened on 17 January 1900 and then seated 630 persons. It cost £5,000 (of which Sir David Salomons, Bt, of Broomhill, gave £3,000) and was the first municipal theatre to be built in England under the Local Government Act of 1894. The poster to the right of the gate advertises a film-show of the funeral of the late King Edward VII and the proclamation of King George V, which dates the photograph to Summer 1910. Sadly, the impressive cast-iron and glass portico at the front of the hall was removed in 1977, the façade was altered and rendered and the trees have long gone, so the exterior has lost its Victorian charm. However, it is well-used for a wide range of events and continues to be a great asset to the town.

Royal Victoria Hall, Southborough.

7 The Old Folks Dinner in the Royal Victoria Hall was an annual event between the wars, and there were many entertainments throughout the year, including theatre productions and pantomime. However, as can be seen from this photograph, the interior was rather plain and the floor was level, which may have been fine for dancing but made it difficult for those at the back of the auditorium to see the stage well. The Town Council has done much in recent years to improve the decor and facilities, and there is now a (removable) stepped floor to give a good view of the stage.

OLD FOLKS DINNER AT SOUTHBOROUGH JAN. 1928.

8 This aerial photograph, postmarked November 1925, looks north over most of the area which was known in Victorian times as Bright Ridge. In the bottom left-hand corner is Rosemead (see No. 9) and the small field above it was the tennis club until about 1950. The large field on the left now holds Southborough Primary School. Christ Church can be seen just to the left of centre, near the top, whilst at top left is the then ground of Southborough Football Club, which swept all before it in the early 1920s. Houses now cover the allotments and football ground, but the cast-iron gates to the latter may still be seen in situ.

S.F.S. SERIES   SOUTHBOROUGH, FROM THE AIR.   PROSPECT ROAD, EDWARD STREET AND FOOTBALL GROUND   No. 2262

9 Rosemead Darby and Joan Home for Aged Couples, which stands on the corner of Speldhurst Road and Prospect Road, was run by the Salvation Army from just after the First World War, when this photograph was taken, until about 1970. It was converted into private flats in the early 1980s.

DARBY AND JOAN HOME. SOUTHBOROUGH.

10 This view, postmarked September 1915, looks westwards from London Road down Holden Park Road to Christ Church (the small spire of which is just visible). Originally named William Street in 1860, after the builder who put up many of the houses, it presents a different scene now. All the trees have gone (the very last was removed in 1979) and there are normally parked cars, nose to tail, all down the right-hand side. Somehow, the left side usually remains clear.

11 Taken before the First World War, this photograph shows a typical backstreet of Southborough 'New Town', the late Victorian development west of London Road. The grocery store of John King, marked by awnings, is now G.H. Major & Son, butcher. Sgt. Albert Mitchell, who as a private in the 13th Light Dragoons took part in the Charge of the Light Brigade at Balaclava on 25 October 1854, later joined Kent County Constabulary and lived for a number of years at No. 20 Norton Road.

NORTON ROAD, SOUTHBOROUGH. J.R. 1007.

12   Prospect Road marked the western boundary of Southborough 'New Town' until the break-up of the Broomhill Estate, soon after the Second World War, provided land for a large number of council houses to be built still further west. At that time, Southborough had the distinction of having more council houses *per capita* than any other town in the country. Here we see some of the solid, respectable, semi-detached Edwardian villas built for the increasingly prosperous townspeople.

Prospect Road, Southborough.

57

13   The High Weald has been affected by freak weather on a number of occasions over the years, but the terrible hail-storm of 25 May 1922 must have been one of the more serious. Next day, the Kent & Sussex Courier reported that perhaps the most amazing incident took place at No. 82 Springfield Road (shown here). The basement kitchen faces Edward Street. A whirlpool occurred on the spot and hailstones were swept down from each side of Springfield Road and Edward Street into the kitchen through the sloping garden. The weight eventually became so great that a com-plete window frame, over four feet square, was forced away from the masonry. The stones swept in, the table rose by degrees with cups and saucers, jug of milk etc. all intact, and the fireplace was completely covered. Later it took eight men to remove the stones, which were reliably estimated to weigh no less than seven tons.

Hailstones, after the storm At Southborough. May 25 1922.

14 Christ Church, Prospect Road, was built in 1870-71 at a cost of £2,390 as a chapel-of-ease for the poorer residents of the Bright Ridge area of Southborough, who would otherwise have had a half-mile walk past the stinking tanyard and over the rough Common to reach St. Peter's Church. Built in a very early English style, it originally had 350 sittings but, even so, had to be enlarged in 1887. The yew tree in the foreground is now so large that it almost obscures the church from this aspect.

15   Although Christ Church had to be enlarged in 1887, ninety years later it had become a little too large for present-day congregations and the opportunity was taken in 1979 to partition off the western end to provide a popular day-care centre run by Age Concern. In an attempt to make the interior a little more 'user-friendly', the pews and, very recently, the polished pulpit and priest's chair have been removed else-where.

Christ Church, Southborough.

Dee's Pictorial Series.

16 The Speedwell petrol station opened for business in 1926 on London Road, opposite Springfield Road. It stood on land carved from the garden of St. Andrew's Park, as the many trees in the background show, and continued in business until changing hands in the 1940s. It is now a Shell petrol station. Note the advertisement on the right of this photograph, of about 1930, which offers petrol at 1/3d per gallon (is just over 6p!). The trade price is even less, at 1/1d. It is clear, from the people waiting, that this spot was also a bus-stop.

THE PETROL STATION, SOUTHBOROUGH.

17   Known for generations as Stemp's Farm, later Dudeney's, the original timber-framed hall house dates from the late 16th century and was probably the home farm of Southborough Hall, which stood on the other side of London Road. Though much restored over the years, the interior has a wealth of oak beams, and two enormous back-to-back stone inglenook fireplaces. The cellar also incorporates a natural spring, providing the house with its own running water, which was also used for cooling churns of milk from the farm. It is believed that a family of Huguenot weavers occupied the house in the 17th century, adding a room at the back high enough to take their looms. During the late 19th century, an owner added tile facings to cover the exterior and these were not finally removed until after 1926, when the original half-timbers were revealed once more. It ceased to be a farmhouse in about 1928 and opened as The Weavers Tea Rooms in 1930, including Wynne's Cake Shop.

THE WEAVERS TEA ROOMS, LONDON ROAD SOUTHBOROUGH.

18 The Weavers Tea Rooms, opened in 1930, used to expand into the garden during the summer months. The garden was quite attractive, having a stream and rockery, a see-saw and a miniature golf-course. However, the tea rooms cannot have been a financial success, because by 1936 they had become a social and residential club for ladies and gentlemen, paying an annual subscription of 5/- (25p). The Second World War put a stop to that and the building became a Canadian officers' mess. After the war, it re-opened as the restaurant we know today.

A CORNER OF THE TEA GARDEN
THE WEAVERS SOUTHBOROUGH.

19   Originally built in about 1870 and then known as Southborough New Hall, it had an imposing front, flanked by two wings. We see here the south wing. In 1891, it was taken over by Reverend Reginald Bull as a preparatory school for boys intended to go to Eton or Harrow, and re-named St. Andrew's School, with its own playing fields, swimming pool and chapel. The stables were converted into a gymnasium. One pupil at least is known to have achieved fame in later life; William Clark-Kennedy, who boarded there in 1891-1893, won the Victoria Cross in France in August 1918, whilst serving with the Canadian infantry.

St Andrew's, Southborough.

20 During the night of 8 February 1919, the south wing of St. Andrew's School was entirely gutted by fire. The night was so cold that the water froze to the firemen's uniforms and the fire appliances, being of the obsolete manual type, could not supply enough water pressure. The Headmaster was so disheartened that he moved the school to Hammerwood, near East Grinstead. The north wing had better luck, remaining as housing until being pulled down in 1970.

St. Andrews, Southborough. Destroyed by Fire. Feb 8ᵈ 1919.

21 The swimming pool of St. Andrew's School continued in use as such for a few years after the school itself had moved away in 1919, but it deteriorated over time and finally became an emergency water supply during the Second World War. It was then filled in.

22 The Old Hall, which stood opposite The Weavers on London Road until it was demolished in 1968, looked as though it originally dated from the late 16th century. However, it was a Victorian reconstruction on the site of a much older building of which a drawing dated 1828 is known.

The Old Hall, Southborough.

36

23 This view, taken just before the First World War, looks northwards along The Parade, the older area of shops on London Road. Once again we find them nearly all on one side of the road, this time on the east. The nearest store is A.F. Hitch, ironmongers, and next is N.A. Killick's dairy. The building beyond is Sheffield Place, put up in 1865. The shop with an awning is Gough & Co., general stores, which was created in 1910-11 from the Crown Inn next door when the latter was reduced in size. Note the distinctive covered balcony, which still exists, running above the first two shops.

London Road, Southborough

24   Just a little further along The Parade, this photograph taken in about 1910 shows clearly the divided footpath, the inner half belonging to the property (which explains the protruding front garden) and the outer half belonging to the council. To the right of the girl in maid's uniform can be seen a pillar-box. This stands outside what was then Paine, Smith's second baker's shop (and post office) and was erected in 1906 at the request of Mr. George Paine, but only on condition that he himself paid half (£3) of the cost of setting it up. Ahead lies the Broadway and Sceptre Hill.

26, London Road, Southborough.

25 This postcard, one of a series of twelve winter scenes made in about 1910, looks back along The Parade towards Tunbridge Wells. The second shop along is G. Mercer, fruiterer, and next is Fielder & Jarrett, newsagents, who were prolific publishers of postcards between 1900 and 1920. Over 225 numbered postcards of Southborough and High Brooms are known, together with a considerable number of unnumbered ones of private houses, presumably specially commissioned, all 'real photographs'. The shop sticking out, with a quaint balcony above, is Wiles, hairdresser, followed by a watchmaker and jeweller and then C. Hall, fishmonger, whose awning sign can just be made out.

3. LONDON ROAD, SOUTHBOROUGH.

26   Our last look at The Parade, in about 1905, shows the Imperial Hotel on the left, offering private and commercial accommodation and a meeting place for the Buffaloes (RAOB). Built in 1859, it was the main competitor of the Hand and Sceptre Hotel (see No. 42) but had to work hard to persuade the petty sessions to grant it a full licence, which they did in 1861. Neither of the entrances visible in this photograph is in use today. Next door can be seen the Parade Bakery of J. Appleton, which was taken over by Paine, Smith in 1906.

SOUTHBOROUGH. THE PARADE.

27   John Wesley himself preached at Little Bounds (then known as New Bounds), at the top of Sceptre Hill, four times between 1762 and 1774, but Methodists had no permanent chapel in the town until 1845, when one was built just west of The Parade. However, the congregation grew and a new chapel, seen on the left of this photograph taken in 1904-05, was erected in 1871 at a cost of £950. Eventually, it also became too small and a more modern church was built nearby in 1936-37 for nearly £10,000. The old chapel was demolished and two houses were put up on the site, their front doors using the wrought-iron hinges from the old chapel.

16433 LONDON RD & WESLEYAN CH.   SOUTHBOROUGH.

28 This view, taken about 1910, looks from Pennington Road across London Road towards St. Peter's Church (the spire is just visible) and the scene remained unchanged until 1965, when the Pennington Grounds recreational area was created, with a bowling green, four hard tennis courts, a putting green and children's playground.

The Meadows, London Road, Southborough.

111

29 St. Thomas's Church, Pennington Road, was built in 1860 entirely at the expense of Mrs. Sarah Pugh, on land gifted by her. She also gave endowments and the grand total of her generosity was over £4,000. It is not clear now why it was thought necessary to build a new church only 400 yards in a straight line from St. Peter's Church on the Common, itself consecrated only thirty years before, but it seems that the main consideration was that St. Peter's was too 'low church', and also that a request for the choir to be robed was turned down. Mrs. Pugh must have felt strongly about something to have given so freely.

SOUTHBOROUGH (near Tunbridge Wells).
St Thomas Church. — LL.

30 St. Thomas's Church needed enlargement by 1879 so 72 seats were added to the north (left) aisle, and the south transept was added in 1889, giving a further twenty 'free' seats. The pulpit and font are of Caen stone, and the church is floored with black and red tiles.

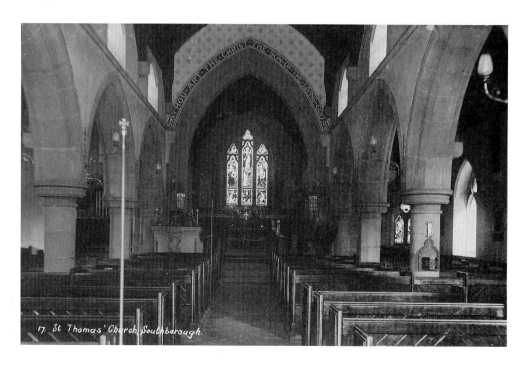

17. St. Thomas' Church, Southborough.

31 The generosity of Mrs. Sarah Pugh to St. Thomas's Church, Pennington Road, continued when she paid for and built the vicarage on part of her own garden in London Road. This gloomy building became redundant by 1950 and was sold to St. Augustine's Roman Catholic Church, Tunbridge Wells, and used for worship by Roman Catholics until 1972, when it was demolished and the present Church of St. Dunstan was built on the site.

St. Thomas' Vicarage, Southborough

32 Along Pennington Road, beyond St. Thomas's Church, stands the Old Dairy, a listed 17th century cottage, now much altered internally. The view north-eastwards from behind this house, down the Colebrook valley to Hadlow, is perhaps the finest in South-borough.

PENNINGTON RD. SOUTHBOROUGH.

33 The Misses Crother gave up their large home at 24 Pennington Road to be used by convalescent servicemen in the First World War and it was entitled Voluntary Aid Detachment (VAD) Kent 94. There were two or three other such temporary hospitals in Southborough throughout that war, and wounded troops in their blue uniform with red tie were a frequent sight on the streets.

V.A.D Kent 94 Crothers Hospital, Southborough.

202.

34 Another large house used as a convalescent hospital during the First World War was Park House, standing on the bend of Park Road. It had been a boys' preparatory school from the 1890s until being requisitioned on the outbreak of war. After the Armistice, it was acquired by the Buffaloes (RAOB) who ran it as an orphanage between the wars, when this photograph was taken. Note the buffalo horns over the front door. After the Second World War, it became a Kent County Council children's reception centre, but was demolished in the 1970s.

R.A.O.B. ORPHANAGE SOUTHBOROUGH.

PHOTO BY ALEC BROOK.

35   No. 12 Park Road, known as Ashburnham House in 1893 and run as a ladies' school, had been converted into furnished apartments by the outbreak of the First World War. By 1921 it had re-opened as the Summer Court Hotel, as in this photograph, but that closed in 1931. Two years later, it had opened as a nursing home and is now a residential home for the elderly.

12 Park Road, Southborough.   209.

36   No. 19 Park Road, built in the mid-19th century, was the smaller of two attached houses, originally known as Clarendon House. For about ten years before the First World War it was a private convalescent home called The Uplands, but reverted to being a private house after the war, when this photograph was taken. In 1928 it became the Uplands Nursing Home and two years later the Southborough Nursing Home. In 1934, the Home took over the house attached next door (No. 17, which had for fifty years been a doctor's house and surgery) but during or soon after the Second World War the whole building was divided into flats.

Eventually, in the 1980s, it was demolished and a purpose-built block of flats erected in its place.

Uplands, Southborough.   52.

37   Once a timber-framed farmhouse, possibly 16th century, this was divided into two cottages during the 19th century (possibly earlier) but became one house again in about 1931, known as Stuart Cottage, London Road. Originally it lay at right-angles to the road. The solar section forms the kitchen of the present house. There used to be an unusual bus-stop sign nearby; a kerb-stone was engraved with the letters BSH (Buses Stop Here), but it disappeared during extensive roadworks in 1992.

Cottages, Southborough.

38 Taken from just outside Stuart Cottage, London Road, on a stretch known as The Broadway, this early view looks up Sceptre Hill to the right and Church Road to the left. The fountain was erected in 1886 to honour Dr. William Fairlie Clark, the Medical Officer of Health who campaigned successfully for the supply of clean public water (see No. 59). The double shop on the left was a grocer, which had housed the town's first post-office from 1843 until 1886. This is now an antique shop and a restaurant. The large house on the extreme left was built on the site of an 18th century inn, The Bell. Behind the line of trees is the cricket pitch.

Photochrome Co.

Church Road and Fountain, Southborough.

39 This view looks southwards back towards The Broadway and, in the distance, The Parade. E. Hartnup the grocer is just beyond the white lamp-post and further on, where a horse and cart are entering London Road, can be seen the shops of Wickenden Bros., grocers and tea dealers, auctioneers and house agents. At the turn of the century, when this photograph was taken, cows were as likely as boys to wander over the grass right up to the main road.

16053 SOUTHBOROUGH FROM THE COMMON. TUNBRIDGE WELLS.

40 Postmarked May 1906, this card shows the south frontage of the Hand and Sceptre Hotel only a few years after its massive transformation in 1897. The horse-trough in the foreground was placed there by Sir David Salomons, Bt., of Broomhill, in 1894. The cottage on the right was the gate-house of Ormode Lodge, which was demolished just before the Second World War to make way for The Meadows Memorial School, run by Dr. Barnardo's (as it then was).

HAND AND SCEPTRE, SOUTHBOROUGH, FROM COMMON.

Mockford—Series 24, Copyright.

41   Probably taken from atop the horse-trough, this photograph shows the parade on Hospital Sunday, 2 July 1922, marching south down Sceptre Hill. Led by the Town Band and the Town Fire Brigade, the contingent included a Queen and her attendants, ex-Servicemen, Scouts and decorated floats, whilst men with buckets milked the spectators of their spare cash. The route went all round the houses, and people at upstairs windows were invited to drop money down drainpipes held over the collecting-buckets. These parades were a highlight of the year and were vital for the running of local hospitals until the National Health Service took over in 1948.

Hospital Sunday at Southborough 2-7-22.

42 The Hand and Sceptre Hotel, pictured here pre-1905, was built as a private house in 1663 and became an inn in 1728. From 19th century photographs, it was a solid, four-square building until about 1897, when the Lord of the Manor and owner, John Deacon of the banking family, had it re-built and transformed. It had been a posting house for coaches travelling to and from London until 1845, by which date a train service had reached Tonbridge and coaches then merely connected with that. The licensee in 1896-97, William Wallace, was also Agent-General of the Royal Niger Company. He was recalled to duty in 1897 and became Acting Governor, Northern Nigeria, from 1900 until 1910, and KCMG! The Hand and Sceptre has been associated with cricket on the Common for over two hundred years, and is still the headquarters of the Southborough Cricket Club.

LONDON ROAD, SOUTHBOROUGH.

Mockford—Series 23, *Copyright.*

43 Although several inns in the town serve meals at the bar, only the Hand and Sceptre Hotel has a dining-room, and here it is in its 1920s glory. The hotel has a tradition of accommodating meetings, for example, the monthly Manorial Court Leet from 1728, the cricket club, the Oddfellows Lodge and the Rotary Club. It is also said to be haunted, and patrons have in the past reported seeing the ghost of a young girl.

Coffee Room, Hand & Sceptre Hotel, Southborough.

44 The War Memorial, overlooking the cricket pitch, was dedicated on 13 February 1921 in memory of 207 officers and men of Southborough and High Brooms who gave their lives in the First World War. One particular tragedy, the sinking of HMS Hythe after a collision with HMS Sarnia whilst approaching the Dardanelles on 28 October 1915, accounted for one officer (the heir to Sir David Salomons, Bt., of Broomhill) and 35 men of the local field company Royal Engineers. After the Second World War, the names of a further eight officers and 36 men were added.

45   The earliest recorded cricket match on the Common was scheduled for 22 July 1794, though there is no confirmation that it was actually played! The earliest published reference to a club at Southborough was in 1821. The small but beautiful ground on the Common has been important and popular in Kentish village cricket; visiting teams have always liked playing here, not least for the hospitality. Plans are in hand to extend the pitch a little, to the south.

View from Hand & Sceptre Hotel, Southborough.   7.

46 St. Peter's Church was built in 1830 by Decimus Burton for John Deacon of Mabledon Park. Previously, worshippers had to go to Bidborough, Tonbridge or Tunbridge Wells. Originally it had a squat tower and an entrance on the east side facing the cricket pitch. Its altar was, unusually, at the west end. In 1866, a short broach spire with four belfry windows was added and the entrance moved to the north side. Then, in 1883, it was extended by Ewan Christian, the present much taller, shingle-clad spire replaced the short one and the clock was added in 1884.

ST. PETER'S CHURCH SOUTHBOROUGH.

Mockford—Series 26, Copyright.

47 St. Peter's Church, seen here from the north-west, a less well-known aspect, had a National School attached, which was built in 1852 for 180 children. The main school room stands on the right of this picture, taken well before the First World War. Enlarged several times, by 1898 the register had 550 pupils, both boys and girls (in separate classes), and the school was remarkable locally for having music classes, physical exercises and for having some lessons outside under the trees in summer. It continued as a primary school until 1969, when the present primary school opened in Broomhill Park Road. After a period of use by part of West Kent College, the school buildings are being re-opened for pre-school and nursery children in 1997.

48 A few yards north of the Hand and Sceptre Hotel, London Road, stands a pair of cottages originally built in 1786-87 as a school for fifty poor boys and girls from the locality, on land gifted by Lady Smythe of Great Bounds and paid for by the Trustees (one of whom was Reverend Charles Wesley) of the estate of the late Reverend Edward Holme. The headmaster's salary was then £30 per annum. This photograph, taken before 1909, shows the schoolhouse on the right and the master's accommodation on the left (now Wesley Cottage and Windy Edge respectively). By 1880, only boys were admitted, but the school closed in 1888. When it re-opened two years later, it was as a technical school for up to 24 girls only. By 1909, the headmistress's salary had risen to £100 per annum, plus free accommodation, but Holme School closed for good in 1916, due in part to the opening of the Tunbridge Wells County School for Girls in St. Johns.

49 Manor Farm (now Manor House) stands at the corner of Vauxhall Lane and London Road, to the north of the town. The 'Manor' was that of Southborough which, in 1790, was acquired by the Earl of Darnley. At that time, Manor Farm was held by James Alexander Snatchall and it lay either side of Vauxhall Lane for 500 yards, then along the north side of Vauxhall Lane for another 1,000 yards. It totalled just over 79 acres, mostly arable fields. The farmhouse had definitely become a dairy by 1886, but probably much earlier, and was run by the Tucker family from about 1912 to about 1953. The dairy then went out of business and the house was left empty and abandoned until 1968, when it was re-occupied as a private house, as it is today.

Manor Farm, Southborough.

50   Just across London Road from Manor House stands Bounds Park Lodge, seen here in about 1910. Built in the mid-19th century in neo-Elizabethan style, it was the main entrance to Great Bounds, a grand mansion which was demolished in 1958. Both the lodge and the gate piers are listed buildings, separately. The lodge is now free of ivy and its stonework can be seen better.

Boundes Park Lodge, Southborough.

138.

51 This photograph of the south front of Great Bounds, which stood to the north-west of the town, was taken about 1914, when the estate was probably at its best. The owner at the time was Mrs. Harland, of the ship-building family, but the estate dates back to before the early 14th century. The earliest parts of the building seen here began to go up towards the end of the 16th century, after Elizabeth I granted it to her kinsman, Lord Hunsden. The estate passed into the hands of the Smythe family soon after, then to the Earl of Darnley in 1790 and to the Hardinge family in the early 19th century.

Great Boundes (South), Southborough.

177

52   Here are the north front and entrance of Great Bounds in about 1914. Erasmus, the Christian humanist and writer (1466-1536), is said to have stayed at the house in the early 16th century, when Sir Thomas More was the tenant, and to have preached on several occasions at Bidborough Church nearby. In 1938, the Reliance Fire and Accident Insurance Corporation took over the house as its headquarters. During the Second World War a large hutted camp was erected in the grounds for staging troops (later taken over by homeless squatters) but eventually, in 1958, the house was demolished. The estate was sold off for private housing, though at least two properties from the old estate remain standing amongst the newer houses.

Great Boundes, (North), Southborough.

180.

53   The Great Bounds Oak, seen here in about 1914, remained after the estate was sold off in 1958 and it stood outside No. 44 Bounds Oak Way for another ten years or so. Eventually it was declared unsafe – perhaps its roots were not given enough space – and it had to be felled. Its girth was 26 feet at a height of 5 feet. It was reputed to be 1,000 years old at its fall, one of the ten oldest trees in the United Kingdom. It has been replaced by a young and healthy oak.

Great Boundes Oak, 500 years old, Southborough.   184

54 St. Catherine's, in Church Road, seen here in about 1911, has an 18th century frontage which conceals an earlier house. John Keble, founder of the Oxford Movement in 1833, stayed here with his collaborators, Manning and Pusey, some time in 1830-1833, when the house was the parsonage of Reverend John Tucker, the first vicar of St. Peter's Church nearby.

St. Catherine's, Southborough.

55   Originally, this building was a late 18th century woodshed owned by a John Carter, who improved it to use as a dwelling. His son, also John, acquired the rights to tenancy in 1827 by what were, in effect, squatters' rights after thirty years' residence. It has been suggested that the property was known locally as Carter's Castle, and this was later shortened to Cat's Castle, as the northern half is now known. Though briefly a school, it has been divided into two residences for over a hundred years (the southern half is called Oak Cottage).

(20) Southborough Common

56   Holden House is a fine late 18th century house, as seen here in about 1910, standing just above Holden Pond. It was for a few years after 1841 the parsonage of St. Peter's Church, but reverted to private ownership by about 1850. It was sold off in 1983 to become a residential home.

23. Holden House, Southborough Common.

57 Holden Corner, overlooking Holden Pond, was quite a separate little community within the town when this photograph was taken in 1896. As can be seen, there were several small shops. For some reason, the area was called Squall's Corner in the Census of 1861. Through the trees on the left can be seen the front entrance of Holden House. The man on the bank is fishing and a hundred years later that sport is still very popular here in the season. A few yards below the pond are the remains of the stone surround of a neglected chalybeate spring.

Southborough. Holden Pond.

58 Modest Corner, another separate little community on the west side of the Common, apparently got its name because the inhabitants were said to be rather immodest in their behaviour. This photograph, taken in about 1904, looks down the path to the old waterworks (see No. 59). Just to the left of centre there is a white pole, which bears the sign of the Beehive Inn, which was open by 1871, possibly well before that. Its earlier years earned it a poor reputation with the Tonbridge Justices but, despite 120 years of good behaviour, in March 1995 it finally lost its licence after complaints by the neighbours, and it is now a private residence.

37088. SOUTHBOROUGH , MODEST CORNER

59   Until 1885, every house in Southborough had its own well or shared one with a neighbour. As the town had no main drainage, most gardens also had a cess-pit and, all too often, the seepage from the latter polluted the former, and there were outbreaks of typhoid. A petition signed by a number of influential citizens in 1880 called for a piped water supply and eventually it was decided to take water from the springs in Bentham Wood. A pump house, with pumps driven by a pair of gas engines, and an engineer's residence were built at the foot of Bentham Hill, seen in this photograph of about 1910. The waterworks were officially opened on 3 June 1885, and the water was pumped to a reservoir holding 100,000 gallons on land behind the Holme Endowed School (see No. 48). Demand soon outstripped supply and a new pumping station was opened at Hayesden on 25 November 1903. The pumping station at Bentham Hill continued to supply water until 1973 but was then closed and converted into a private residence soon after.

Southborough Waterworks.

60 This charming little cottage, the East Lodge of Bentham Hill, was built in about 1830, probably by Decimus Burton, in Tudor Gothic mode. It stands near Holden Pond, at the bottom of Trotting Hill, at the start of a drive nearly half a mile long, now overgrown and scarcely passable.

Bentham Hill Lodge, Southborough.

139.

61   Bentham Hill, seen here facing the south-west frontage in about 1909, was built in the Deveyesque manner by Decimus Burton in 1830-1832, and is considered to be possibly the progenitor of the 'Olde English' style. The owners, the Potts family, made their money from the manufacture of vinegar. However, the house was sold up after the Second World War and was converted in about 1948 into eight flats.

'Bentham Hill' Southborough.

62 The north front of Bentham Hill, photographed here in about 1910, is strikingly different from the other three sides, taking advantage of the sloping ground to include a terrace walk with a low wall above a series of garden rooms. The view towards Modest Corner and the Common is very fine.

Bentham Hill, Southborough.

63 The Common, which is made up of open areas of grassland and mainly deciduous woods, is a local jewel and is now owned by the Town Council as Lord of the Manor. This photograph, taken about 1910, shows that part popularly known as 'The South of France' (because the sun is said always to shine on it!). The houses along Holden Road opposite are of a variety of styles and include, at Nos. 15 and 17, a pair of 18th century cottages.

27. Holden Road from Common, Southborough.

64　This close-up of the eastern end of Holden Road, taken about 1910, is of particular interest because it includes at the extreme left, tucked behind a tree, the forge of Joshua Crowhurst, blacksmith, who had been there since before 1867. This was one of two forges in the town (the other being, appropriately enough, in Forge Road in the 'New Town' area) and it continued in business (under new management) until 1932.

Holden Road, Southborough.

65 Looking northwards from the middle of 'The South of France' on the Common, the background of this photograph from before 1908 includes a row of houses known to older residents as 'Sunnyside', on Victoria Road. Cattle grazed freely on the Common, usually escorted by a teenage boy, before the increase in passing traffic made that too hazardous for all concerned.

Victoria Road, Southborough.   8.

66   Postmarked October 1909, this photograph was taken from a small area of the Common noted for its interesting heath flora and looks towards a very mixed-up cluster of quaint houses including, at the right-hand end, 'Woodcote', a Regency cottage of about 1830.

12. Southborough Common

67 Broomhill, better known as David Salomons' House and now The Salomons Centre, was the family seat of the 1st and 2nd Baronets. An earlier house, owned by the Baden-Powells, was pulled down and replaced in a complex Italianate style in 1850, with several later extensions. This aerial view from the 1930s, looking east, shows the layout well, including the south front and terrace, the science theatre (now devoted more to the arts) built in 1894-1896 to the north of the house, the ivy-covered water-tower behind it and, at the top of the picture, the stables. The estate is now a conference and training centre owned and run by Christchurch College, Canterbury.

AN AERIAL VIEW OF DAVID SOLOMONS HOUSE, SOUTHBOROUGH

R.9609

68   Broomhill was handed over in trust to Kent County Council in 1938, to be used for educational or medical purposes. After occupation by children evacuated from London during the Blitz of 1940, it became a convalescent hospital for wounded airmen. On the creation of the National Health Service in 1948, it became a convalescent home for women, and the south front and terrace seen here were popular for enjoying the sun. This role lasted until about 1975, after which it became the conference and training centre of the Regional Health Authority. This view shows well the water-tower, built in 1876 by Sir David Salomons, on top of which he established an astronomical observatory, though that fell into disuse when he was no longer fit enough to cope with the cold night air.

53542. South Front, David Salomons House, Southborough, Kent.

69   The artificial lake at Broomhill, created in the early years of this century, incorporated a central island and an unusual design which divided the circular pool by low walls into segments. When it was necessary to clean out the lake, the water level was lowered until the walls just appeared, as in this photograph. Each segment was then drained and cleaned in turn, the fish being transferred to a neighbouring segment until the cleaned one was refilled.

The Lake, David Salamons Home.

TBW 4

70 The stables at Broomhill, built in 1890-94, were designed by Sir David Salomons himself in the lay-out and style of a French chateau, to accommodate 21 horses, twelve carriages, a forge and a sick-bay. There were also numerous labour-saving, mechanical devices of Sir David's own invention. This is the only Grade II* listed building in Southbor-ough. When the Regional Health Authority took over Broomhill in 1948, the sta-bles housed a sub-depot of the National Blood Transfu-sion Service until 1995.

54167. The Stables, David Salomons House, Southborough, Kent.

71 Here we are looking back, west-wards, along Yew Tree Road towards London Road and Gallards Close in the 1920s. This road leads to High Brooms and is now considerably more busy with traffic than as shown here. Most of the houses were built between the wars, filling the open spaces which then separated High Brooms from Southborough.

YEW TREE ROAD SOUTHBOROUGH.

22

72   Prior to 1902, High Brooms had no Anglican church of its own, but the growing population needed their own parish and, thanks to the gift of £5,000 by Lady Harriet Leslie Melville, the church of St. Matthew was built, using (naturally) bricks from the High Brooms Brick and Tile Co. This fine church, able to seat five hundred people and impressive enough to lead one commentator to call it a cathedral in miniature, was consecrated in 1902. It contains one particular memorial, a large marble plaque recording the names of those of 1/3 (Kent) Field Company, Royal Engineers, the local Territorial Force unit, who lost their lives when HMS Hythe sank on 28 October 1915 off the Dardanelles.

73 The railway line between Tonbridge and Tunbridge Wells forms the eastern boundary of Southborough and High Brooms. It was built by the South-Eastern Railway Co. in 1844-45, and opened on 21 September 1845. The line was difficult to build and required, among other engineering feats, a viaduct of 26 arches, some 254 yards long, over the Colebrook valley, which stands at the northern end of Powder Mill Lane. There had indeed been a water-powered gunpowder mill in the Colebrook valley, from about 1770 until before 1845, by which date it had become a corn mill – just as well, considering the proximity of the new railway line!

THE VIADUCT, SOUTHBOROUGH.

74   Until 1893, there had been no station on the railway line between Tonbridge and Tunbridge Wells, but in that year, due to the growth of Southborough, a station was opened at nearby High Brooms. Unfortunately, the station was called 'Southborough' until 21 September 1925, when it was sensibly re-named 'High Brooms' in recognition of the fact that the best way to reach Southborough by public transport was by bus along London Road, and this is true today. In this early photograph, later used as a postcard, note the station-master on the down platform and no less than three porters on the up. The High Brooms Brick and Tile Co. (1885-1968) had its own sidings close to the station, so that bricks could be loaded straight onto wagons for delivery by rail to most parts of the country.

15) Southborough Station. SER.
(now High Brooms) 25/4/93.

75 The availability of large amounts of Wadhurst clay at High Brooms made brick-making a rewarding business, providing work for men from near and far. A local firm made bricks on the spot for the Colebrook viaduct in 1844-45 and by 1855 several firms were flourishing. In 1885, the High Brooms Brick and Tile Co. was established close to the railway. The quality was so good that its bricks were in demand across the south of England and were used in the Blackwall Tunnel, Brighton Power Station and later in the Aswan Dam, Egypt. The works also produced terra-cotta plaques, finials and fantastic creatures with which to decorate buildings using their bricks. The company continued to thrive until the 1960s, but a sharp slump in the building trade led to fewer orders and in 1968 the decision was made to close the brickworks. The last of the claypits was filled in, the ground levelled and the area used for light industry. This view, taken in about 1915, looks south-west from the railway, with High Brooms on the high ground behind.

59219. HIGH BROOMS. THE BRICK WORKS.

76   At the northern limit of Southborough, the last building stands prominently on the left-hand side of the main road. It is Mabledon, built in 1805 for James Burton, father of Decimus Burton (who was then aged four), on a wooded hill-top overlooking the Medway valley and Tonbridge. The original building was not large and, in an etching by Peter Amsinck dated 1809, it lacked the many twisted chimneys which may be seen today. They were added, together with an extension to the front façade and the large square north tower, by Decimus Burton when he was employed to make alterations in 1870. Requisitioned by the Government during and after the Second World War, it was not released to the Church Pastoral Aid Society, to whom it had been left by the previous owner, until 1955. After use as a Christian conference centre, it was sold privately in 1992.

MABLEDON TONBRIDGE